I.L.Y. ANYWAY

Dr. Yi

Our tales last night were too exciting,
now you're tired, bed inviting.

Dreams hold tight
   to their last chance.
We rush to school—
   our morning dance.

Tonight we learn, in time so clever,
plan our stories, late nights, never.

We pass spills off without a care, next time, a plate with room to spare!

You draw on walls, in lines and curls,
a sprawling space, your mind's own world.

Ideas burst forth, they just won't quit.
The wall looks odd, not meant for it.

While cleaning walls, our hearts ascend,
a canvas waits for you, my friend!

You come inside, so full of dirt,
with pawprints scattered on your shirt.
A chase with your best furry friend,
until we knew it had to end.

Let's wash up,
  clear the dirt away.
More clean clothes
  for next time we play.

In the stillness of the night,
you wake me 'cause your tummy's tight.

Your coughs and sneezes fill the air.

To feel so sick just isn't fair.

You boldly take that toy apart,
with eager hands and open heart.
Inside, a hidden work of art,
each piece examined, you're so smart.

And when it's time for us to mend,
with love and patience we will tend.

You rise in class with nerves so near,
heart racing, courage held so dear.

You take each step, eyes on the floor.
Some words are missed, you feel unsure.

At home, just us,
no rush to do,
we'll practice gently,
start anew.

Together at the store we stand,
frustration rising, close at hand.
You cannot get what you desire.
Don't hide your sadness, let's inquire.

Big feelings are okay, my dear.
We'll work through all them, have no fear.

At the swing, you feel unwell.
The motion lost its graceful spell.
The playground's loud, it hurts your ear,
you want to leave, and that's quite clear.

A room of faces, quite unknown,
you feel unsure, left on your own.

The laughter sounds, games in the air,
but you stand still, filled with despair.

We'll start with smiles, a kind "hello." Your unease soon is sure to go.

In every hurdle, big or small,
our love stands tall, won't ever fall.
Through every tear, through each pause,
our bond remains without a cause.
In every moment, night or day,
love shines so bright, won't fade away.

Thank you for joining the enchanting journey of
I Love You (I.L.Y.) Anyway. This picture book is a gentle reminder that
children mirror the support they receive from their caregivers, reflecting our
own hearts back at us. Through their innocent eyes, they grow and learn, shaped by the examples we set.
Every child deserves a love that is strong, consistent, and tender: a love that holds them close through every single
challenge. *I Love You (I.L.Y.) Anyway* highlights 10 key moments that illuminate children's unspoken needs,
offering meaningful ways to deepen our connections with them. Together, we celebrate the beauty of
unconditional love, embracing children as they are while they blossom into their unique selves.

"A heartfelt thank you to the wonderful editor, Brooke Vitale, and to thoughtful fiends, Damian Joseph Quinn and Tim,
who generously shared their feedback. Special thanks to the talented artists, Ryan Webb and Arthur.
Your patience and support made this book possible."

-Dr. Yi

William James Collection
williamjamescollection.com
Chicago, Illinois, United States

I.L.Y. Anyway

Age 4 and Up

GUIDING WITH LOVE, PARENTING WITH GRACE.

Copyright @ 2025 by Dr. Yi (Yi Zhang) and The Learning Brand LLC
All rights reserved.

Library of Congress Number: 2025900630
ISBN: 979-8-9907914-2-8

No part of this publication may be reproduced or distributed in any form or by any means without prior
wrote consent from the publisher. Our books may be purchased in bulk for promotional, educational, or
business use. First edition, 2025.

www.ingramcontent.com/pod-product-compliance
Lightning Source LLC
Chambersburg PA
CBRC091135130526
44582CB00036B/175